THE
SALADO
CREEK GANG
Don Kirk

OTHER BOOKS BY
DON KIRK

AVAILABLE FROM THE PUBLISHER
lulu.com/spotlight/sweetwater
amazon.com
barnes&noble.com

*Welcome to Redrock Canyon Territory:
An Old West Resort, Movie Ranch, Entertainment Park,
and Open-Air Living History Museum*

*Barbed Wire, Windmills, & Six Guns: A Book of Trivia,
Fact, and Folklore About The American West*

Discovery Bay

Erika

Hinsdale: The Summer of '58

Cool Short Stories: Psychodramas With A Twist

My Remembrances Of Life At Tompkins Barracks

The Story of Columbia Coloring Book

Western Art Coloring Book Vol I & Vol II

Iron Horse Art Coloring Book

Sundry Art Coloring Book

THE SALADO CREEK GANG

1975-1977
Gunfight Acting Troupe
San Antonio, Texas

Photos By

DON KIRK

Actor

Playwright

Costume Designer

The Salado Creek Gang
A Weekend Pastime
By Don Kirk

Published by
SWEETWATER STAGELINES™
An imprint of
THE OLD WEST COMPANY™
5118 Village Trail Drive
San Antonio, Texas 78218

Tradepaper (ISBN13): 978-1-7320075-1-2
Printed and bound in the United States of America
R2

SWEETWATER STAGELINES™
SAN ANTONIO, TEXAS

The Salado Creek Gang

A Weekend Pastime

By Don Kirk

FORWARD

What would you do if you were out of work for the weekend and had nothing to do? Put on some raggedy-old clothes, grab a leather gun holster and .45-caliber pistol, and then load it with blanks? This small group of western fans did just that...and got paid for it.

This book was put together for those who were there and is a thank you to Paul Wisdom, owner of Ole San Antone, who made it all happen for us Old West Fans.

DonKirk

The Salado Creek Gang
One Version

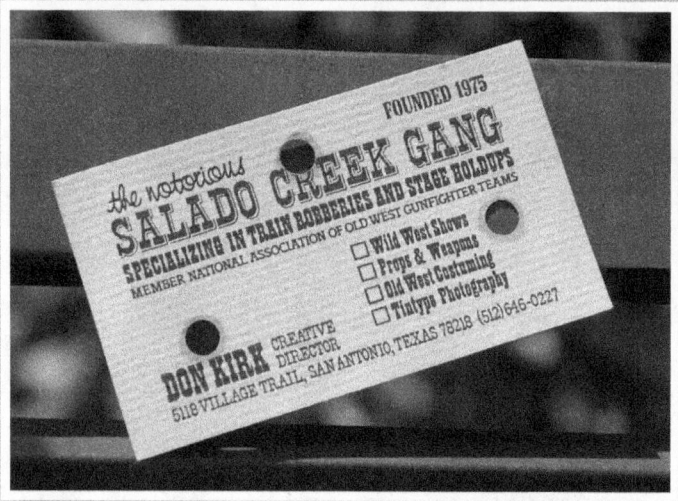

**A Memorable Business Card
Because It had "Bullet Holes" In It.**

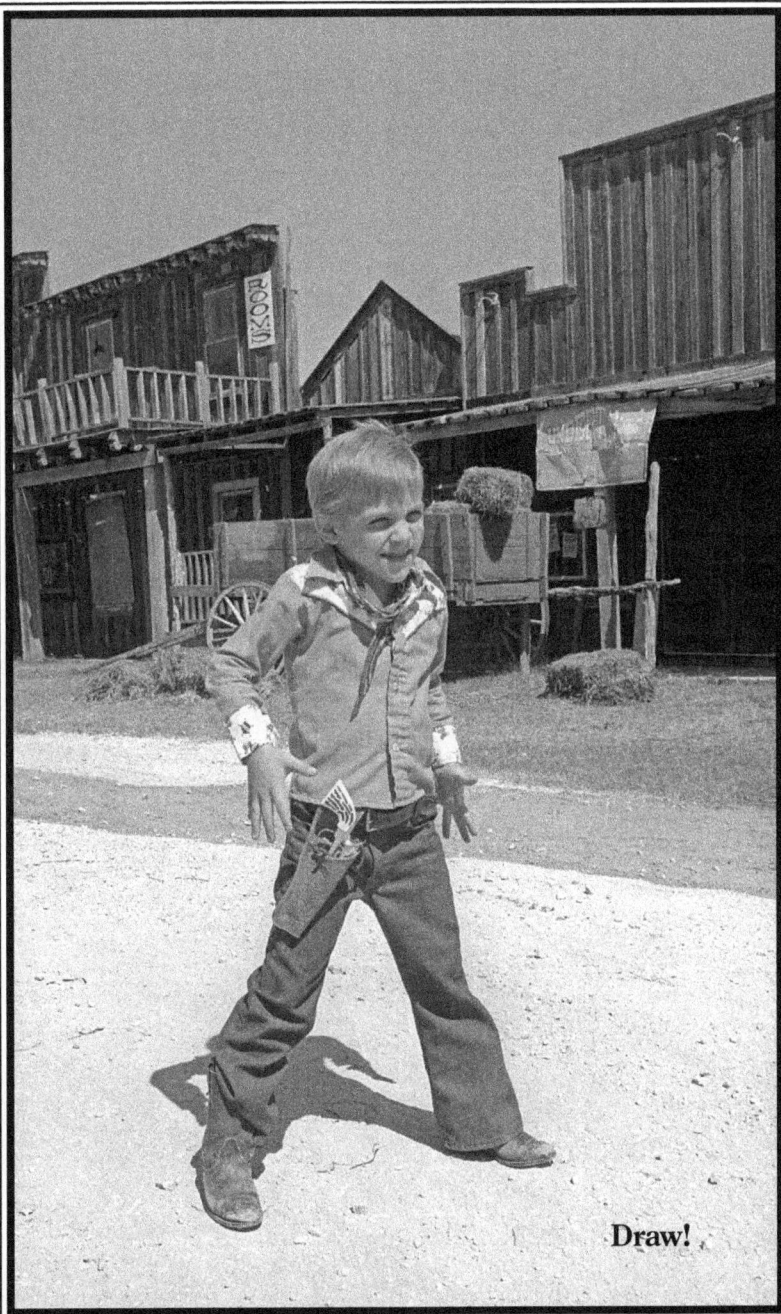

Draw!

Ole San Antone Western Village
San Antonio, Texas

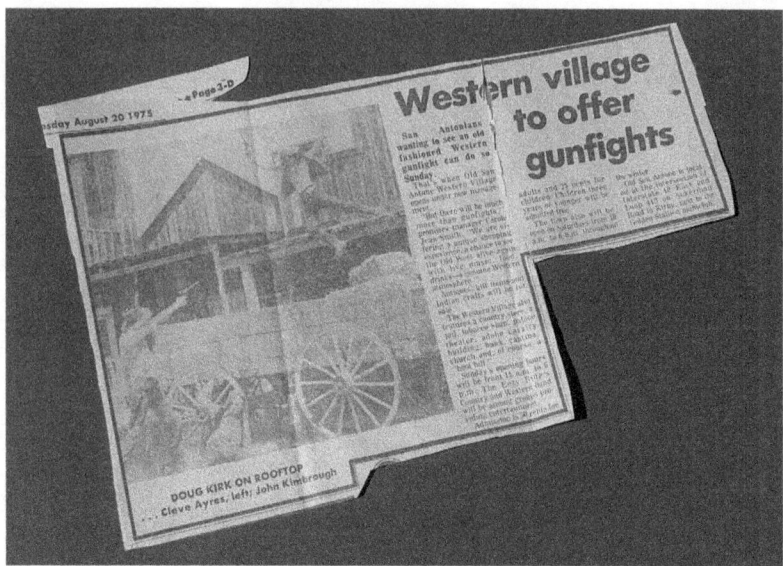

San Antonio News, August 20, 1975

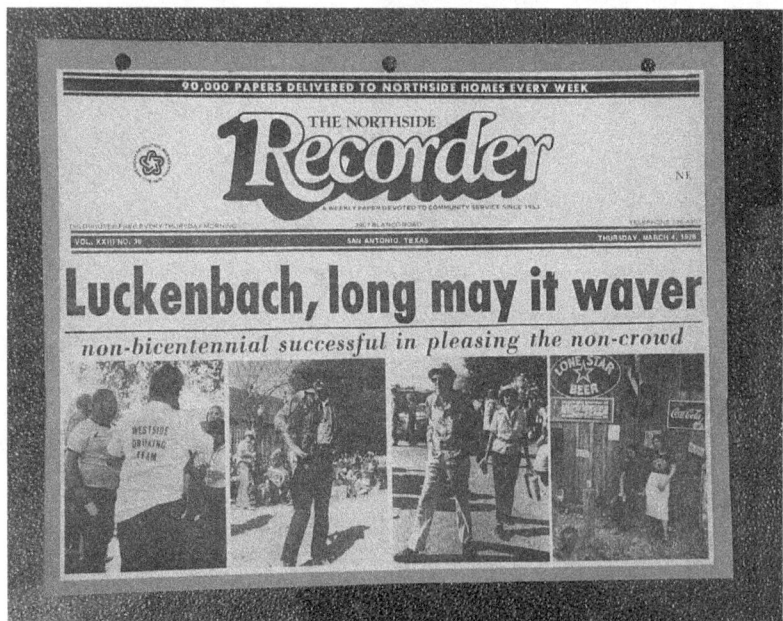

The Northside Recorder, March 4, 1976

Western Village To Offer Gunfights
Wild West Gunfights
Keep Your Hand On Your Pistol

The San Antonio News:

"**Western village to offer gunfights**. San Antonians wanting to see an old fashioned Western gunfight can do so Sunday. That's when Old San Antone Western Village opens under new management. 'But there will be much more than gunfights,' promises manager Carole Jean Smith. 'We are offering a unique shopping experience, a chance to see the Old West alive again with music, food, drinks—a genuine Western atmosphere."

"Antiques, gift items and Indian crafts will be for sale. The Western Village also features a country store, a jail, tobacco shop, palace theater, adobe cavalry building, bank, cantina, church, and of course, a 'boot hill.' Admission is 50 cents for adults and 25 cents for children." —20 August 1975"

The Boerne Star   Thursday, April 1, 1976

WILDWEST GANG COMES TO WINN'S TO SHOP THE REAL VARIETY STORE

**WANTED DEAD OR ALIVE
SALADO CREEK GANG
APRIL 3, 12 Noon to 6 P.M.**

On April 3, a bit of History comes to life when the Salado Creek Gang rides into Boerne to show you how it was 100 years ago in the old West.

This gang, who holds out in San Antonio, comes to town at the request of the Winn's Store. This bunch of outlaws and desperados will be putting on gunfight shows Saturday, April 3, from 12 noon until 6 P.M. Each show is five to ten minutes long, and there will be one show every hour on the hour. All shows will be different. This all happens in the Live Oak Shopping Center in front of the Winn's Store.

The Salado Creek Gang was formed in July of 1975 by Don Kirk and John Kimbrough. With the help of Doug Kirk an organization was formed that has appeared in "Ole San Antonio" in San Antonio, Luckenbach, Texas for their non-buy Centennial, Von Ormy's Bi-Centennial Celebration, and for the Fort Sam Road Runner's Club. Now they come to Boerne. So come to Winn's Store on April 3 and see how it really was a hundred years ago.

NEW SPRING
Assortment Of
Buster Brown Clothes
For Boys and Girls

**APRIL 1 - 3
Boerne Store Only**

BEDDING PLANTS

WILD WEST GUNFIGHTS!

Saturday, June 5
at the Kingsland Winn's Store!
See the Salado Creek Gang stage Wild West shoot outs! Every hour on the hour from 11 a.m. to 4 p.m. Shows last from 5 to 10 minutes each. Each one is different, so see them all!

**FUN!
FUN!
FUN!**

COME A
THE MA
AND REGI

1st Prize - 10"
ing
2nd Prize - Rif
3rd Prize - Lo
4th Prize - Tw
Sel

No Purchas

PRECI
TIME-REL
PLANT F
For all house a
nts. Long la
No Mess
z. Reg. $

ECIAL

ATERING
lc 1 qt.

PECIAL

ARTHEN
NGING B
rative cla
un rope h
tural Sou
inside or

97c

The Boerne Star, April 1, 1976

The Salado Creek Gang

Wild West Gunfights
Keep Your Hand On Your Pistol

The Boerne Star:

"**Wanted Dead Or Alive, SALADO CREEK GANG,** April 3, 12 noon to 6 P.M. On April 3, a bit of History comes to life when the Salado Creek Gang rides into Boerne to show you how it was 100 years ago in the Old West. This gang, who holds out in San Antonio, comes to town at the request of the Winn's Store. This bunch of outlaws and desperados will be putting on gunfight shows Saturday…Each show is five to ten minutes long, and there will be one show every hour on the hour. All shows will be different. This all happens in the Live Oak Shopping Center in front of the Winn's Store. The Salado Creek Gang was formed in July of 1975 by Don Kirk and John Kimbrough. With the help of Doug Kirk, an organization was formed that has appeared in 'Ole San Antonio' in San Antonio, Luckenbach, Texas for their non-buy Centennial, Von Ormy's Bi-Centennial Celebration, and for the Fort Sam Road Runner's Club. Now they come to Boerne. So come to Winn's Store on April 3 and see how it really was a hundred years ago." —1 April 1976

An Abandoned Town...

Or Quiet Before The Storm?

Ole San Antone, Kirby, Texas 1975

The Town On A Quiet Monday?

The Salado Creek Gang
Another Version

The Dressing Room At Ole San Antone

The Salado Creek Gang

The Gang Last Week

Black Bart (Don Kirk, Co-founder)

A year out of the military, and a 6th year of college,
and this is what it brought: playing a gunfighter,
what better pastime.

Always Ready For A Good Gunfight

Larry "Lo" Tucker as "Buffalo" in the Marshal's jail...
and an escape in the offing.

If not by one method, then another: taking John
Kimbrough's pistol.

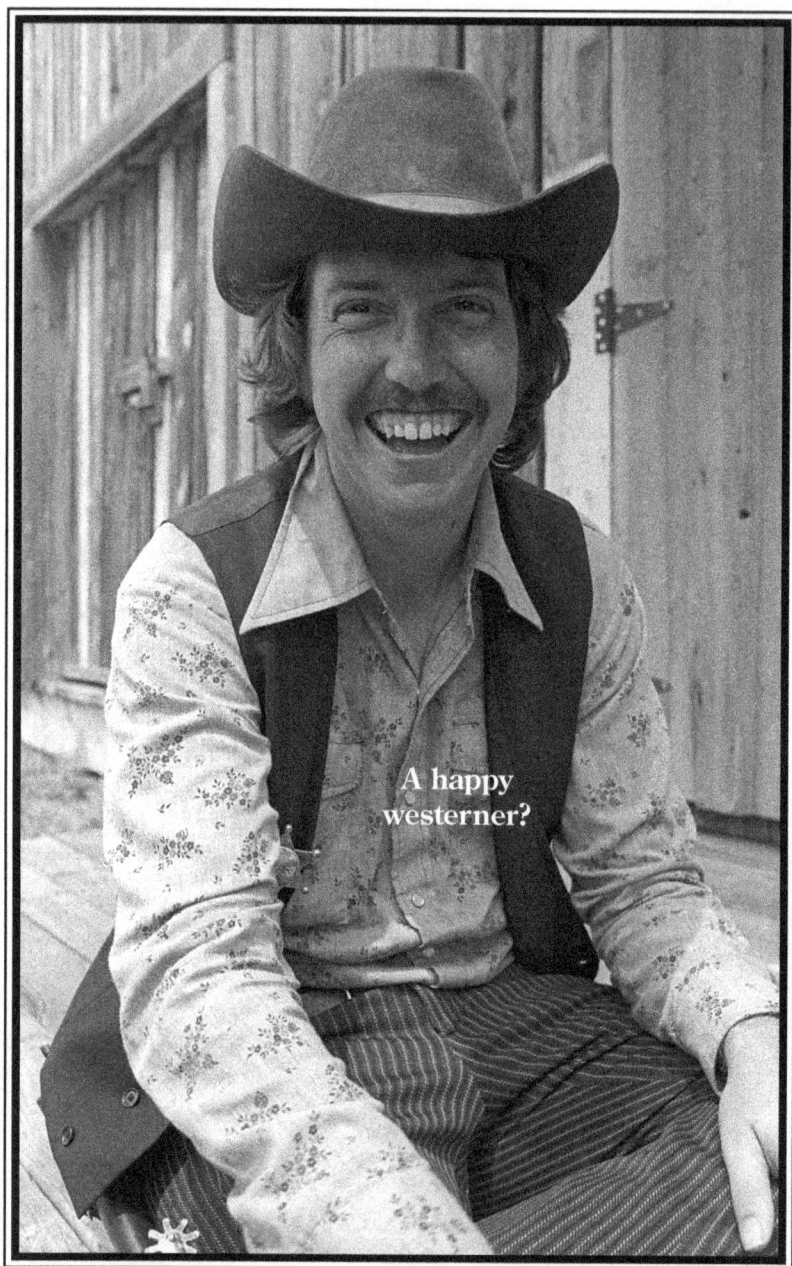

A happy westerner?

John Kimbrough (Salado Creek Gang co-founder)

A Mean, Tough
Westerner?

Shotgun
At The Ready

Buffalo (Larry Tucker)

Dusty (Cleve Ayres)
And Buffalo Driving Stagecoach

Extra Security When Hauling Money Or Gold

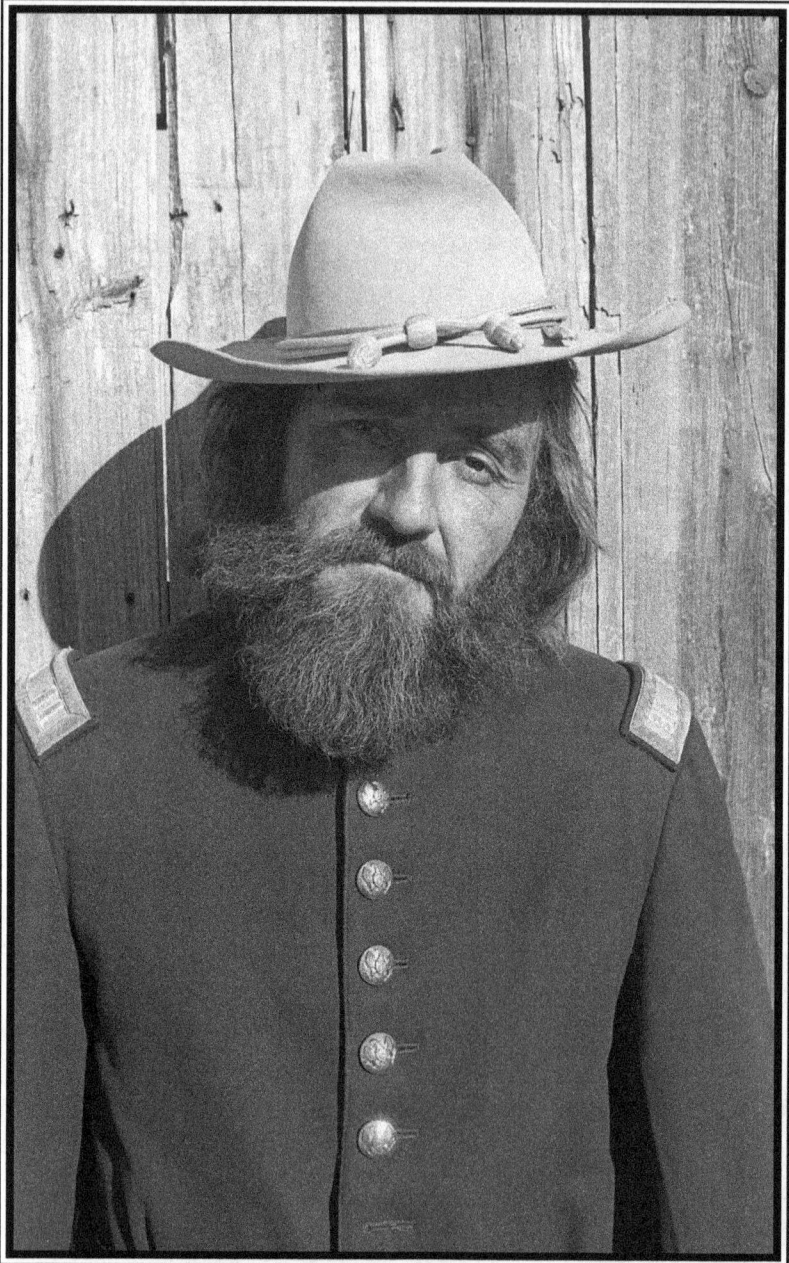

Buffalo As A Union Officer

Buffalo As The Bath House Manager

Buffalo (Larry Tucker) Never Took "No" For An Answer

Dusty (Cleve Ayres) At The Wrong End Of The Barrel

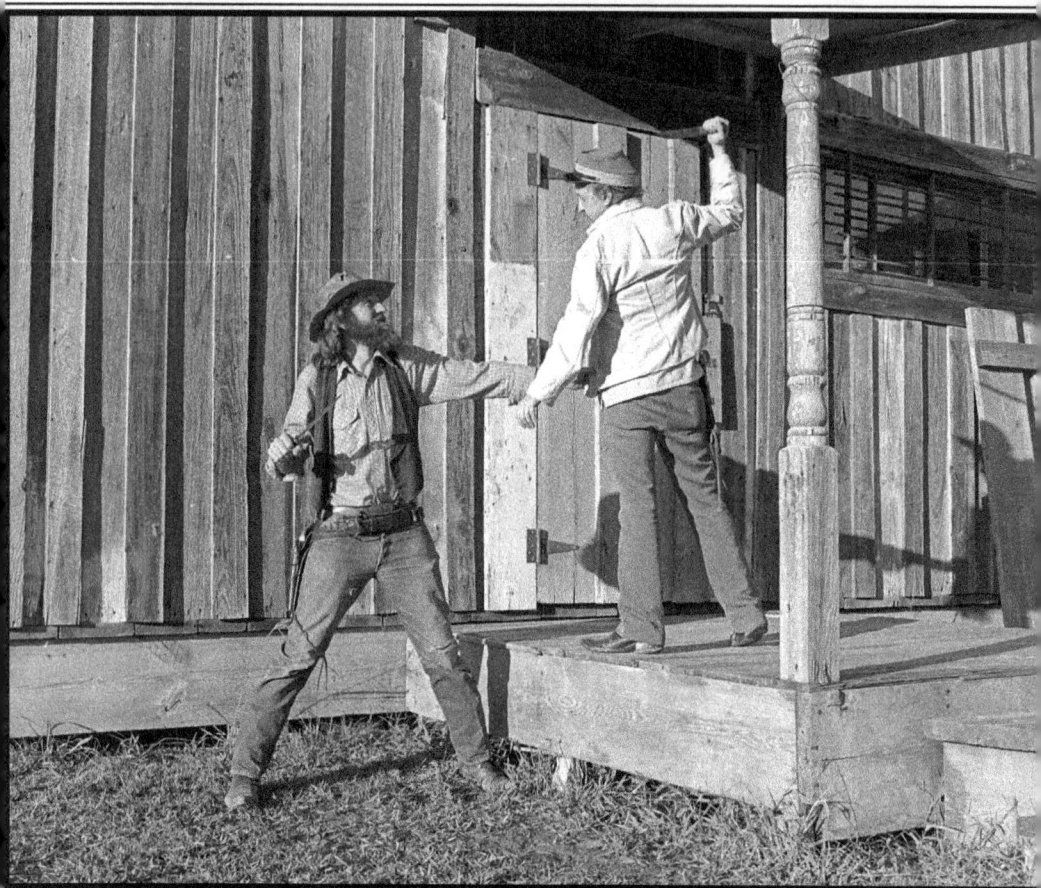

Johnny Reb and Buffalo
In A Knife Fight

(No, The Knives Weren't Real,
Because The Body Was)

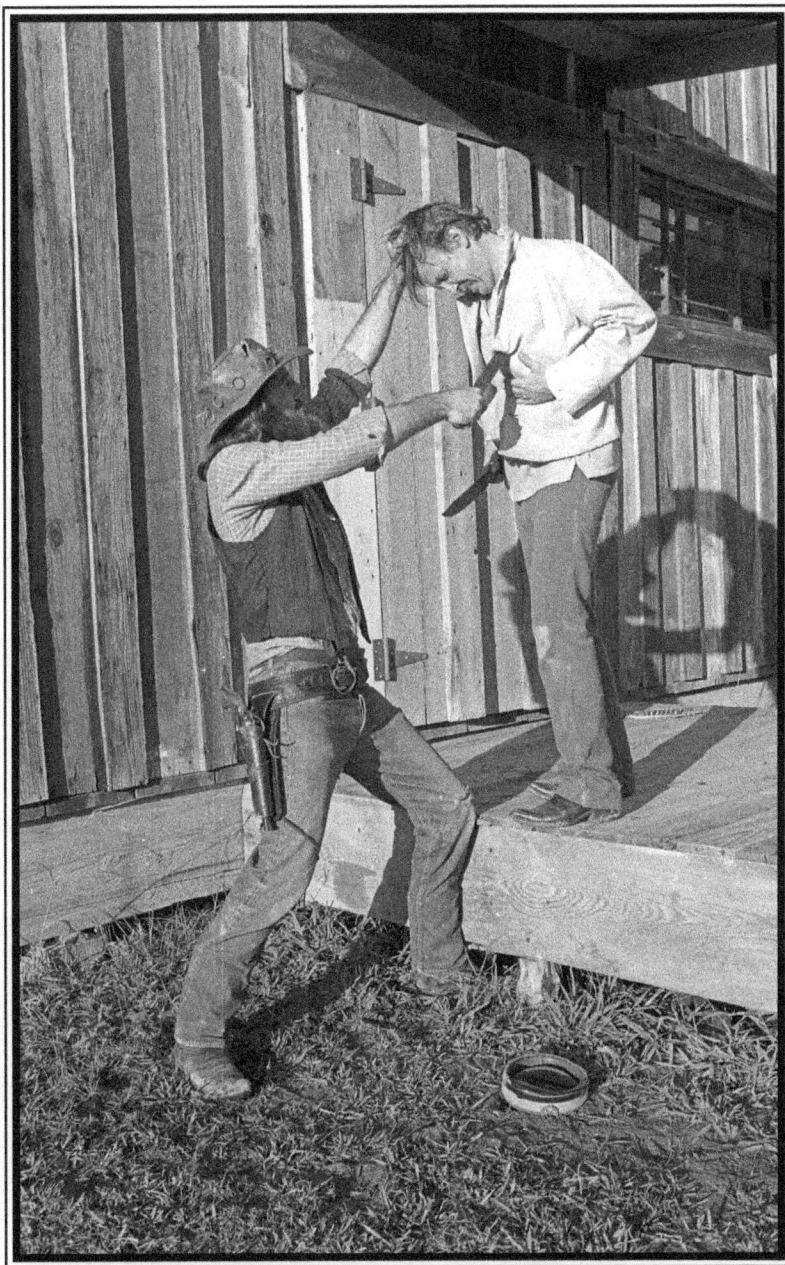

Just As Effective As A Gun

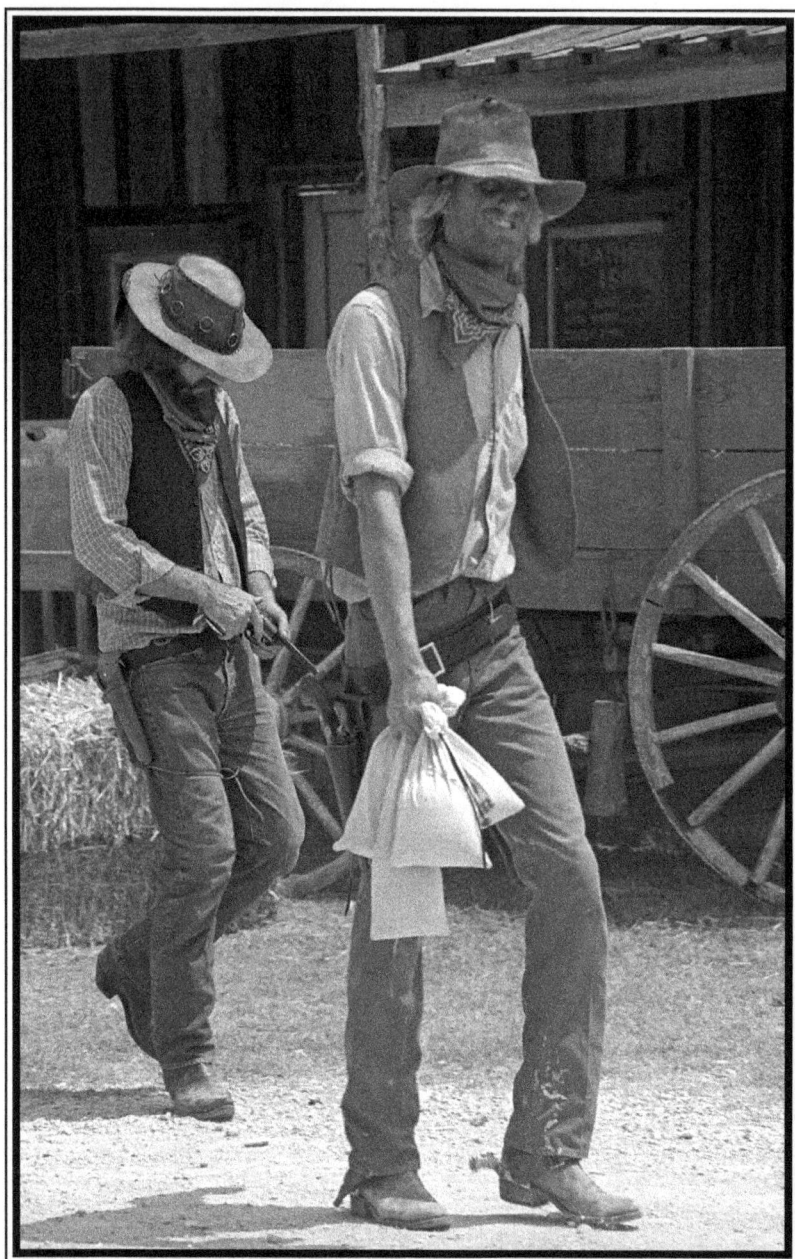

Outlaws, For Some Reason, Love Banks

Dusty (Cleve Ayres)

Dusty And His Girl

Buffalo, In Back, Looking On

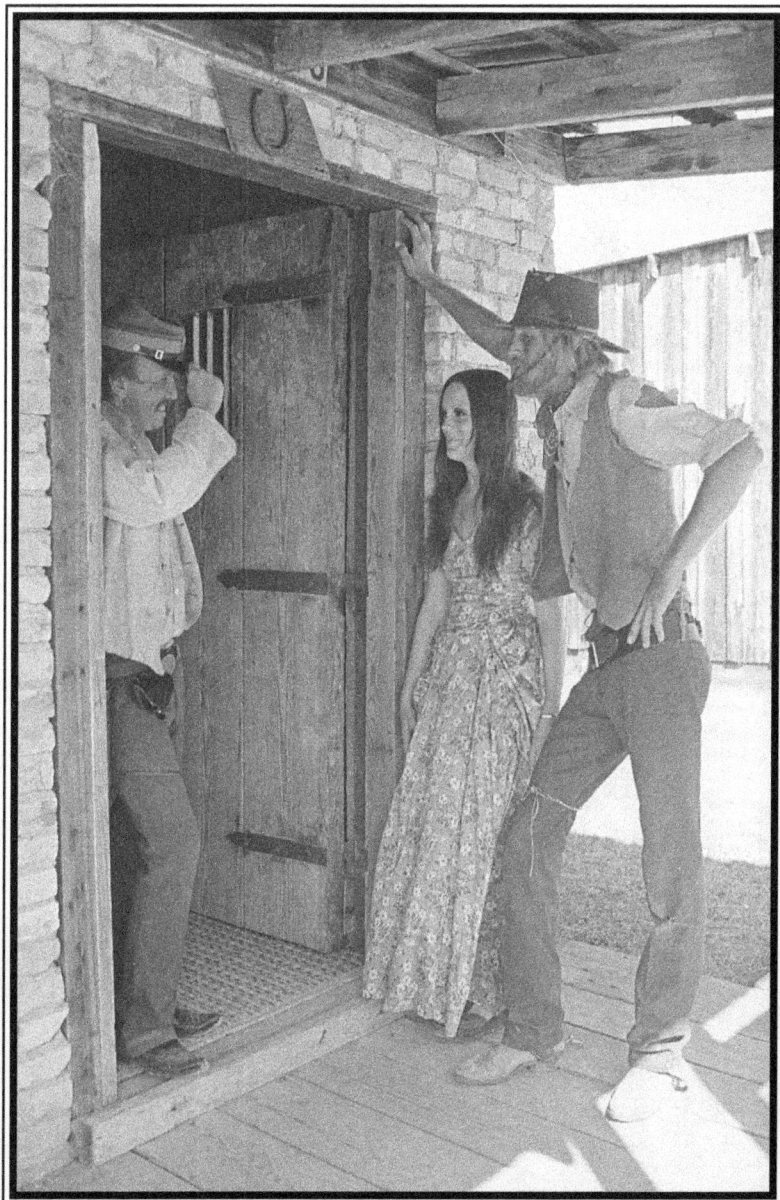

Johnny Reb Meets Dusty's Girl

Reprocess: Print Too Light

Dusty

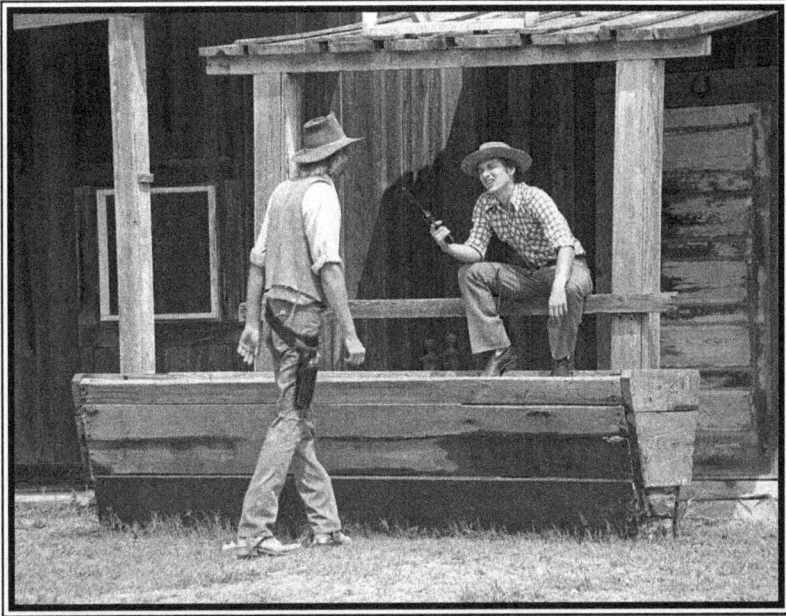

Dusty And The Kid (Douglas Kirk) With His Pistol

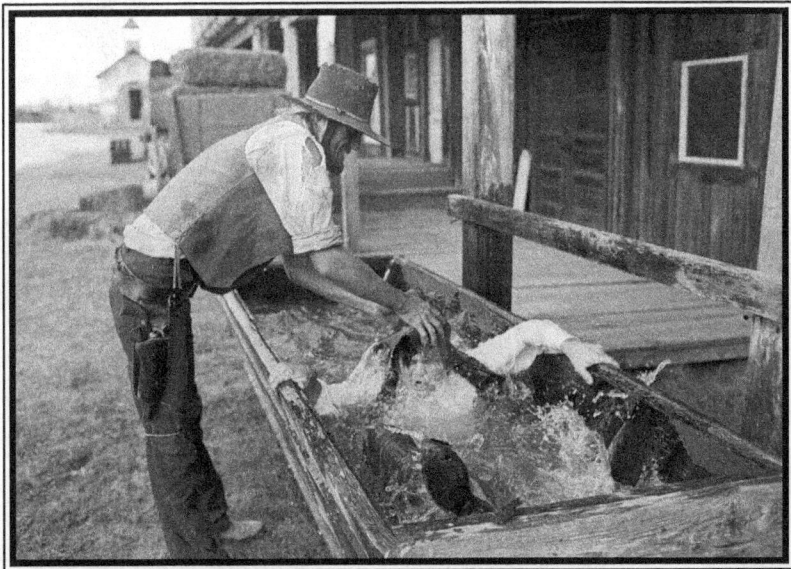

Dusty And The Kid Without His Pistol

Even a Fall From A Rooftop After Getting Hit, Or Shot,
Was Part Of The Show

Man With No Name (Paul Morrison) and he only owned one shirt.

What An Actor Will Do To Hold An Audience

A Kah-pow To Buffalo...

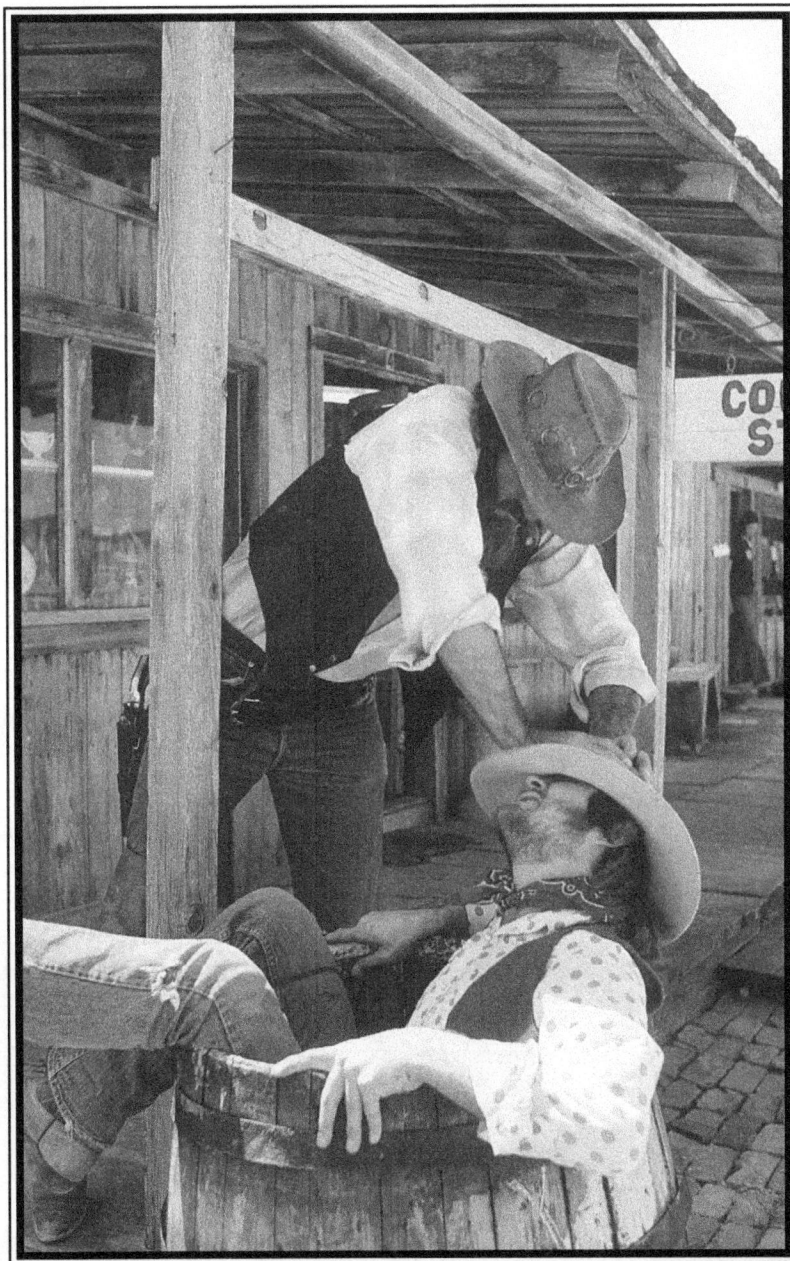

A Water-Barrel Dunking From Buffalo

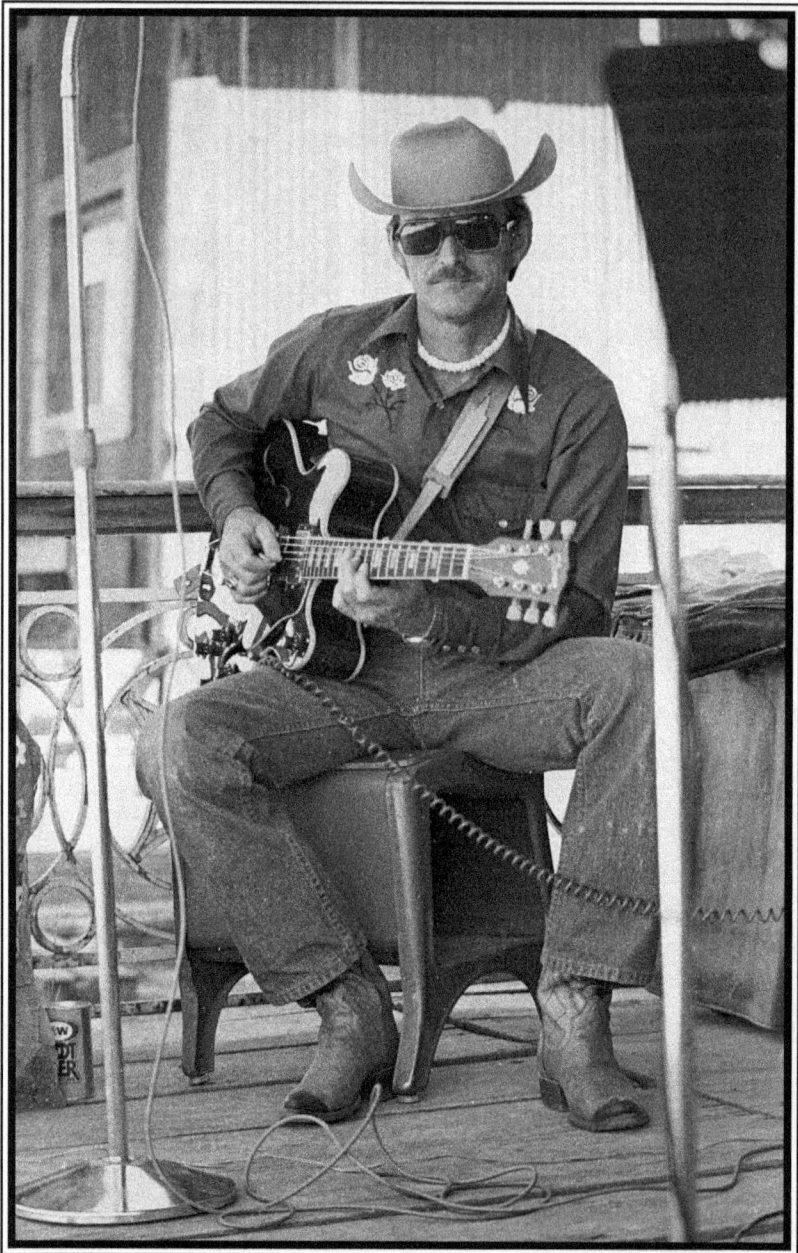

Musicians Were Also A Regular Weekend Event

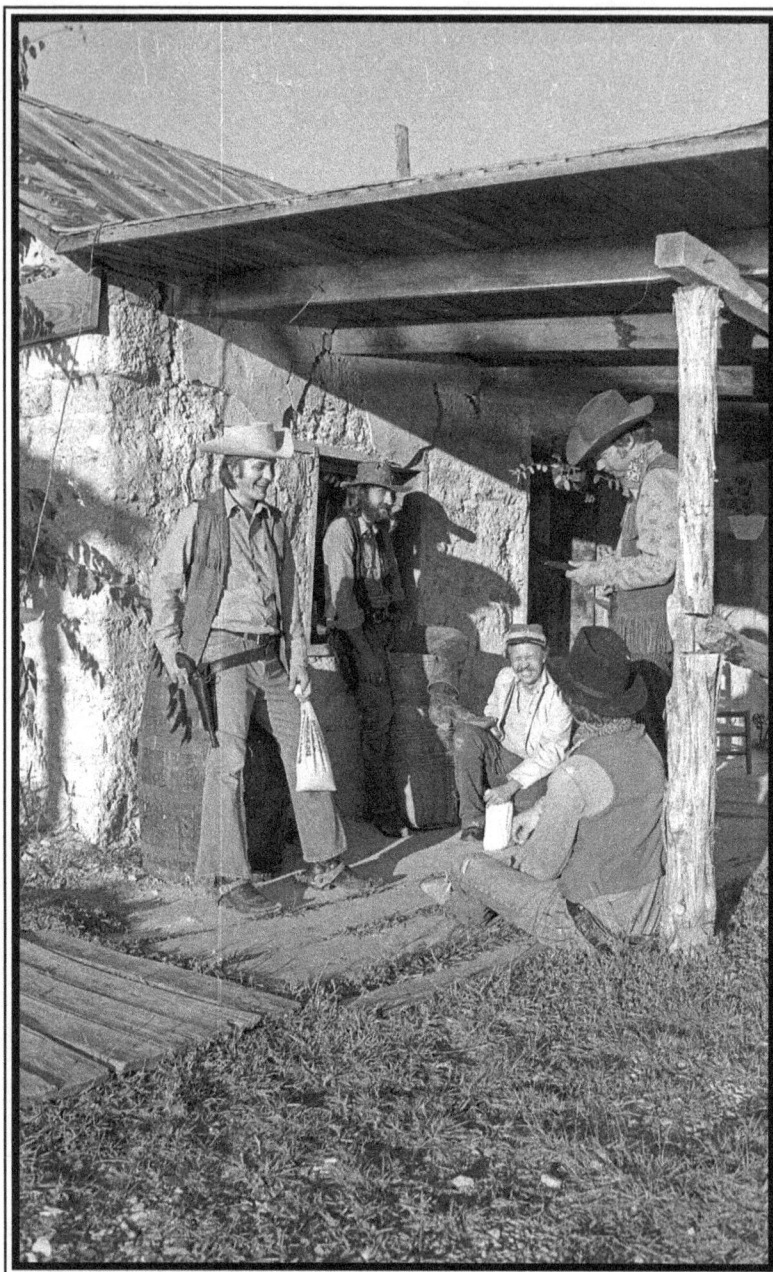

A Rest Break Between Hourly Shows...

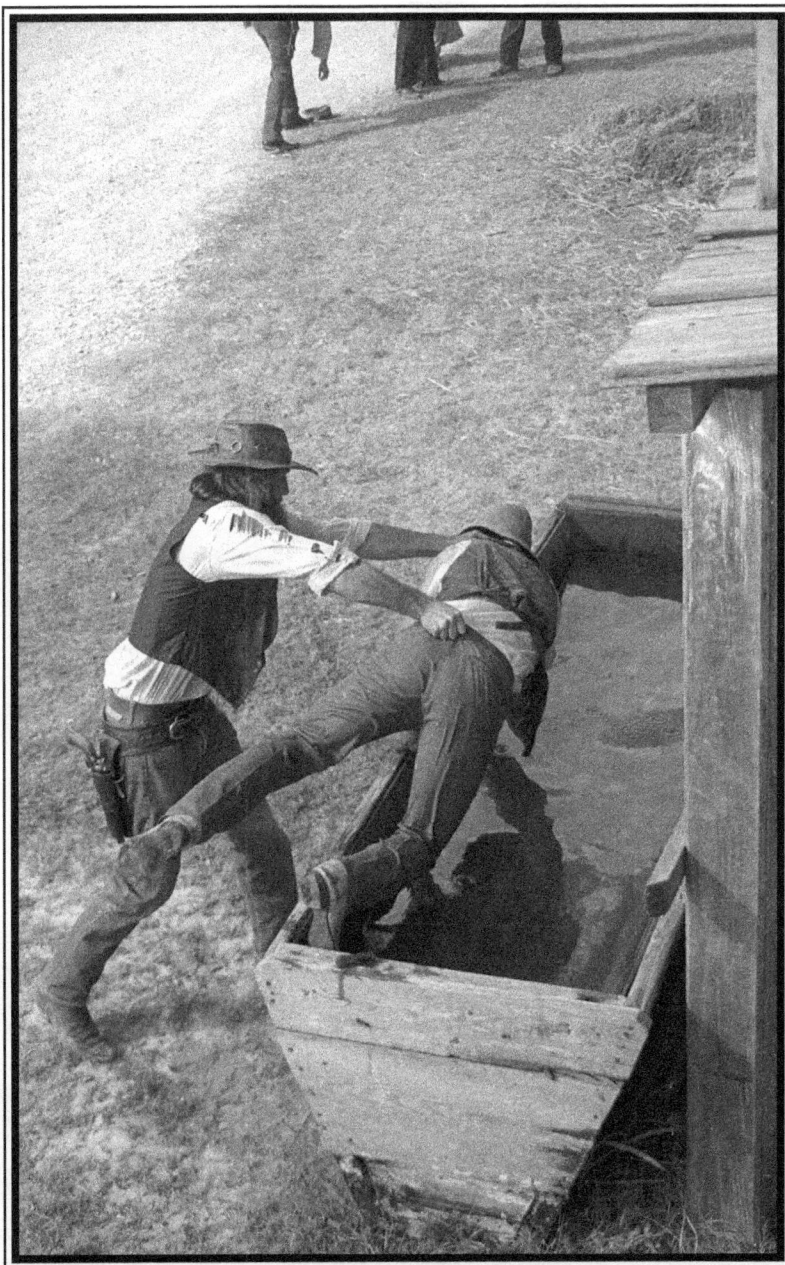

And A Refreshing Drink

Gunfights
Where
Part Of
Every
Show...
Every
Hour

(We Made
Our Own
Blanks)

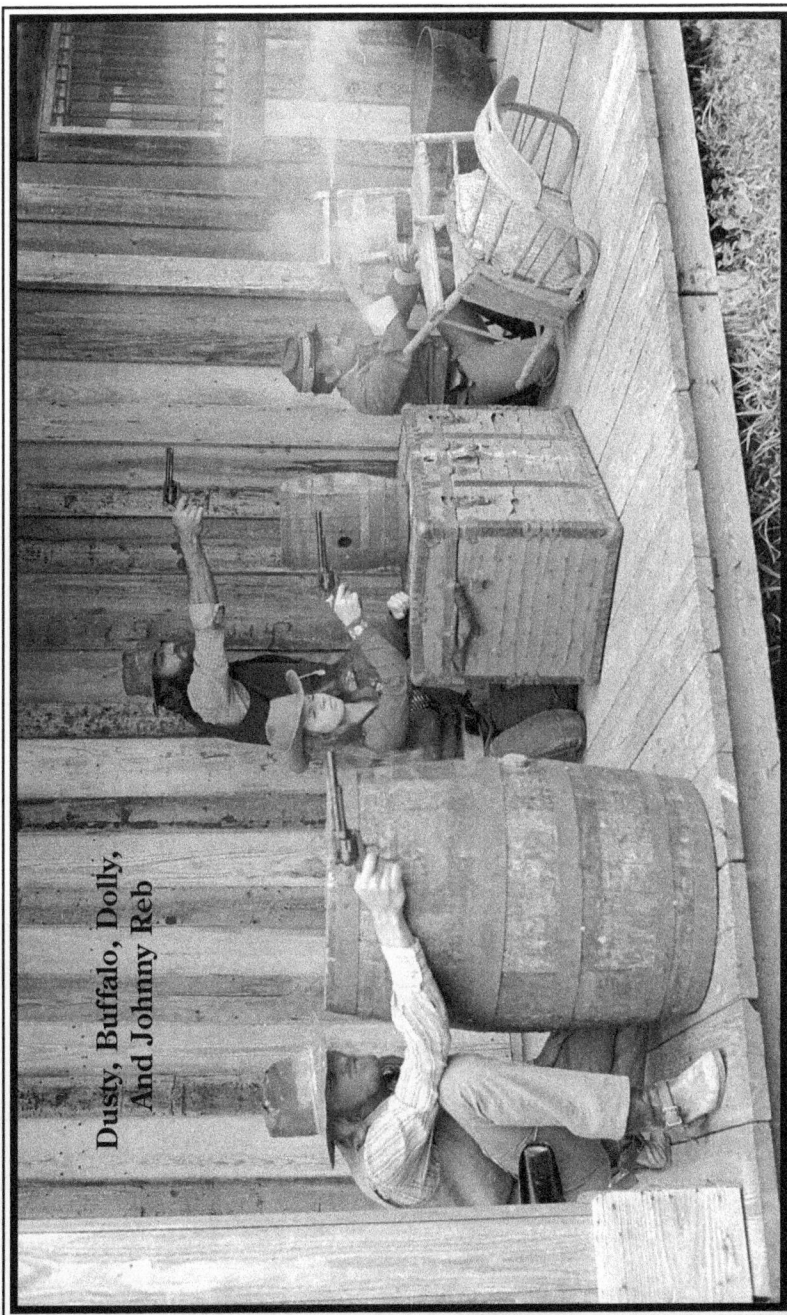

Dusty, Buffalo, Dolly, And Johnny Reb

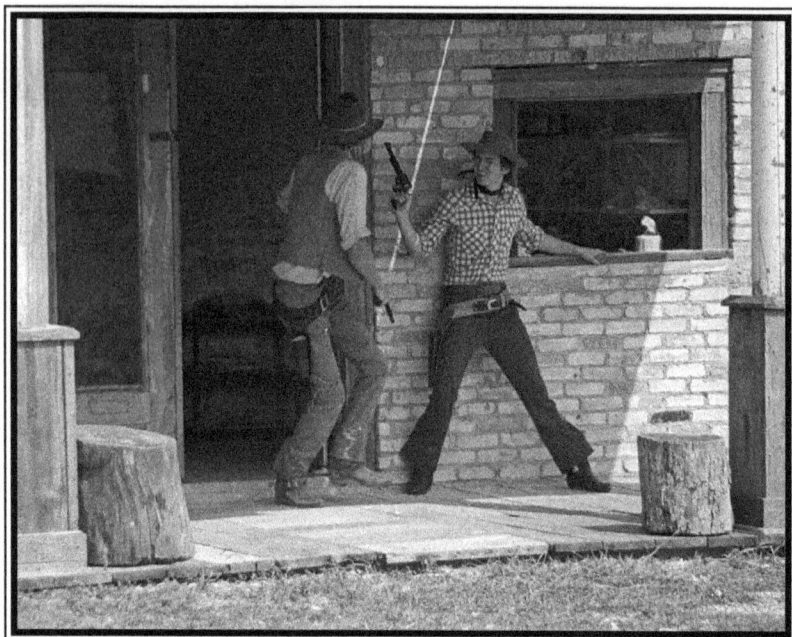

The Kid (Douglas Kirk), Always Getting Into Trouble...

Until His Untimely End

Dolly, The Saloon Owner

Dolly With Her Alluring Smile

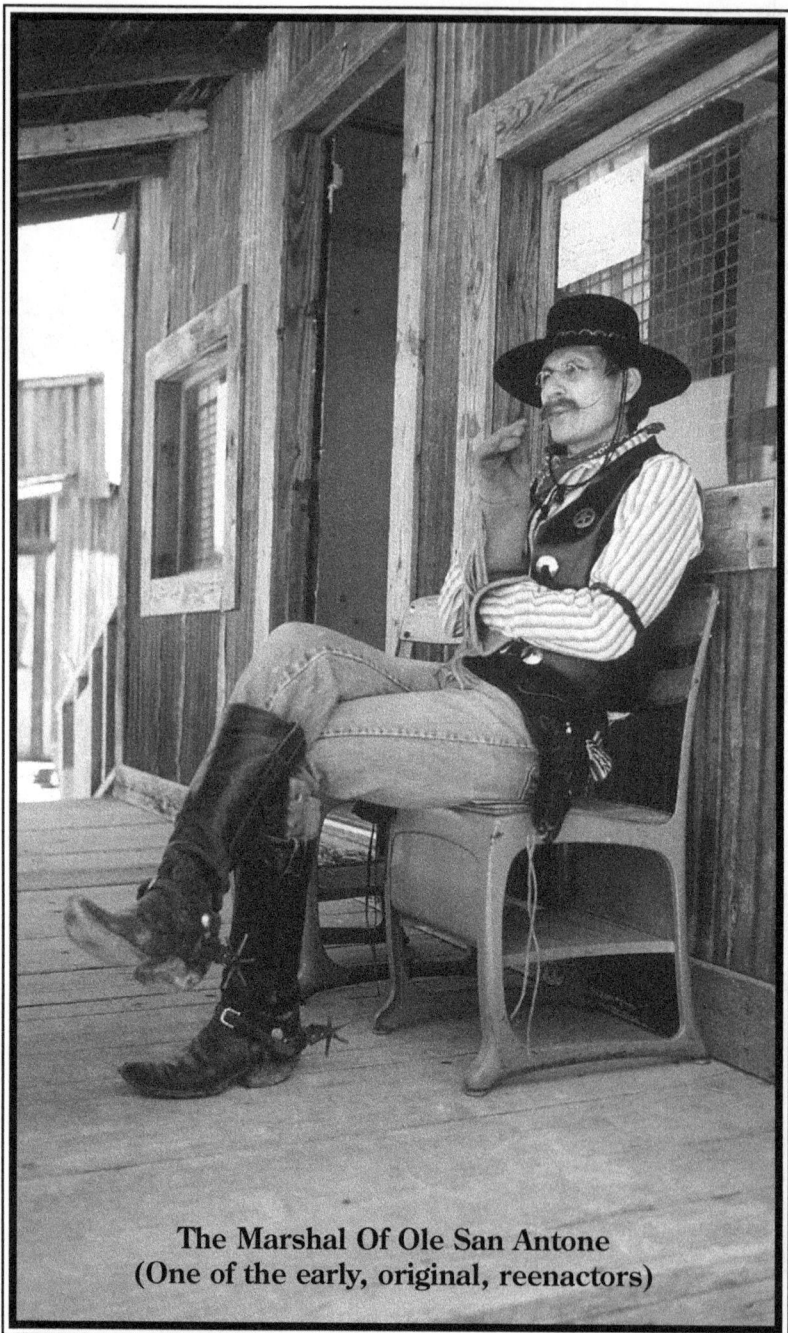

The Marshal Of Ole San Antone
(One of the early, original, reenactors)

Dolly Using Her Two Six-guns

Doug, Valorie Matthews, and Cleve Speaking To Guests

The Kid (Douglas Kirk)

The Marshal OF Ole San Antone (Real Name Unknown)

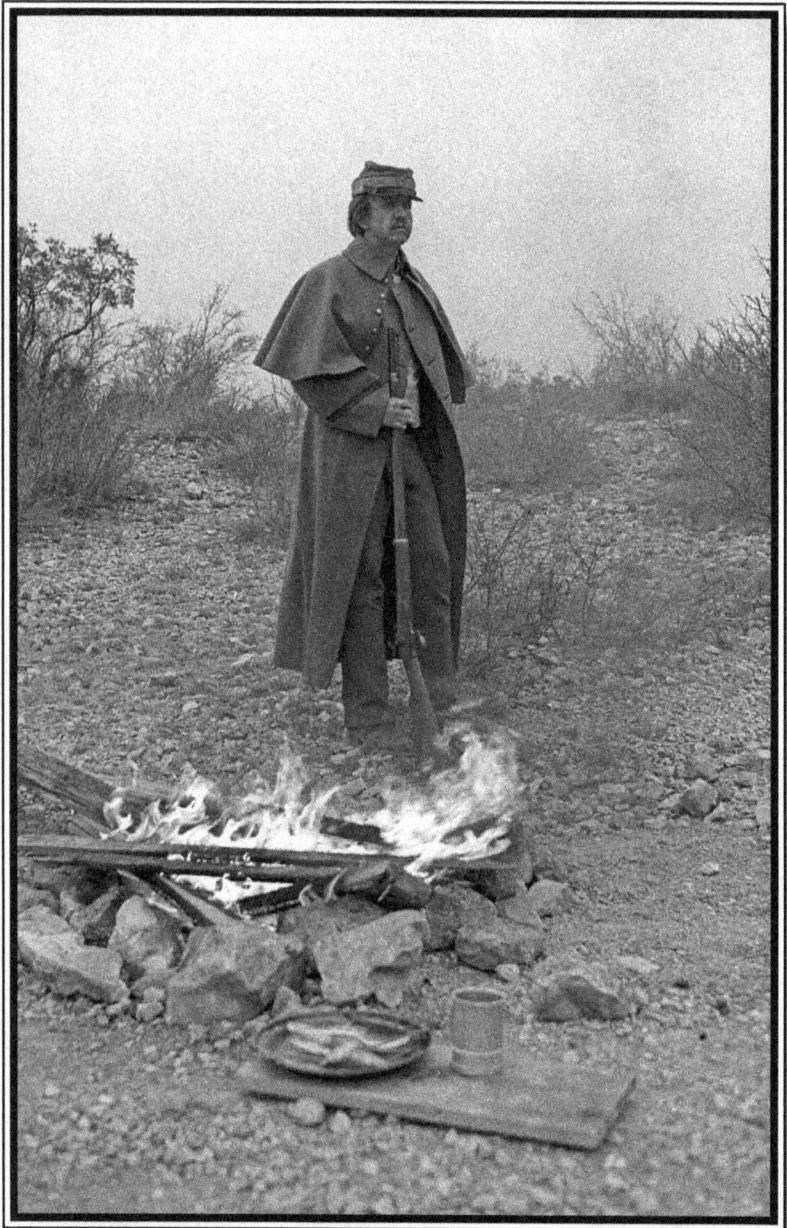

Johnny Reb Of The Confederacy Camp Fire
(Photo taken at Alamo Village, Brackettville, TX)

Wayne Connor, Confederate, and below, as Union Soldier

Wayne Connor, Confederate Soldier

Wayne Connor, Union Soldier

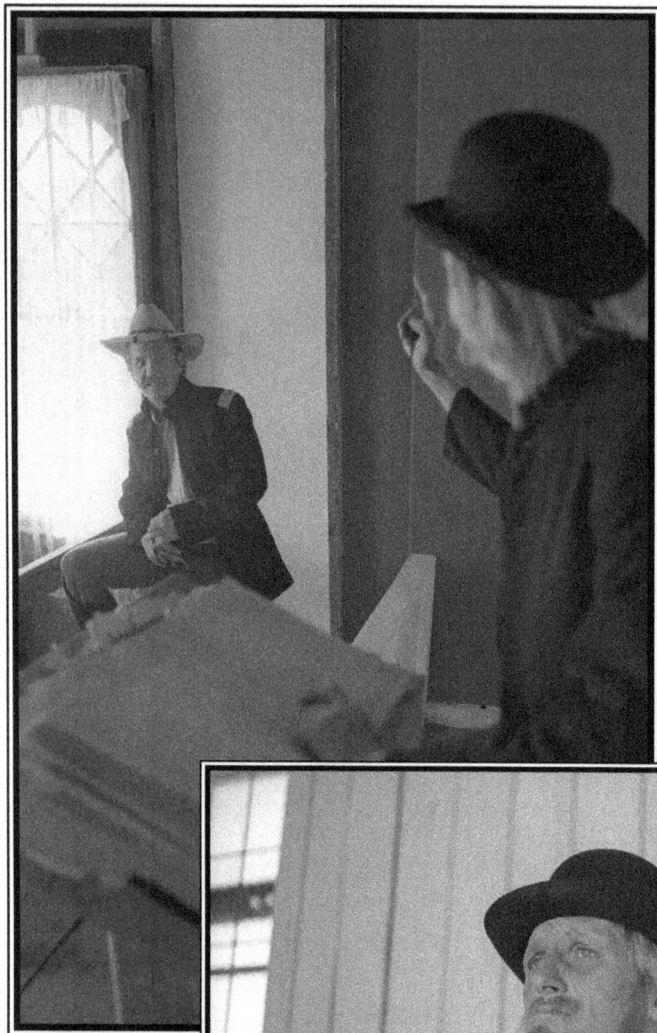

A Union Soldier (Reb) Listening To The Town Preacher (Dusty)

"Do Right Or Get Shot!" Ordered The Preacher

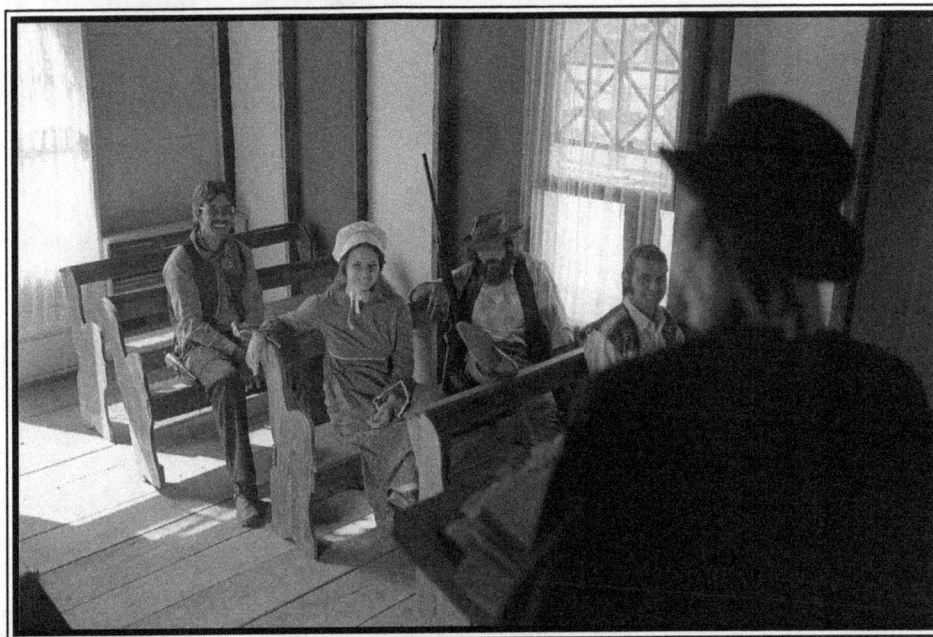

"You Like My Jokes, Do Yah?
I Don't Take 'No' For An Answer."

"Good Sermon, Preacher,
Love That Pistol O' Yourn."

Ole San Antone

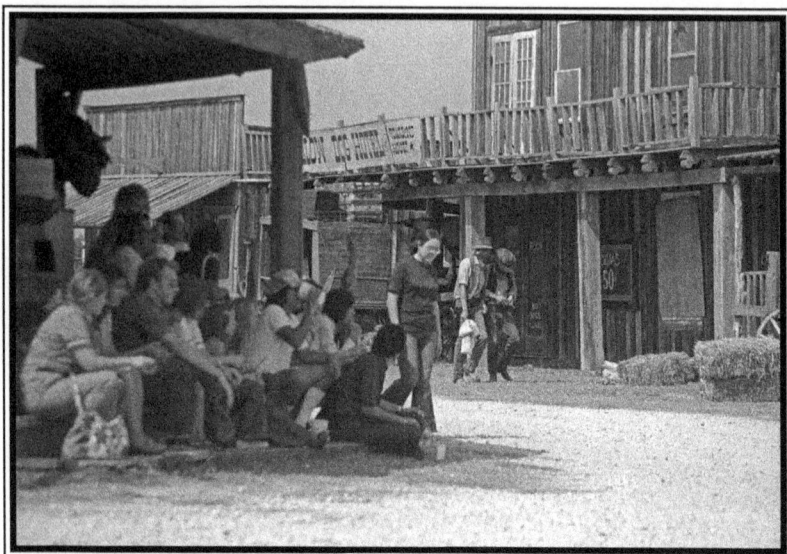

A Small Crowd Ready For A Gunfight

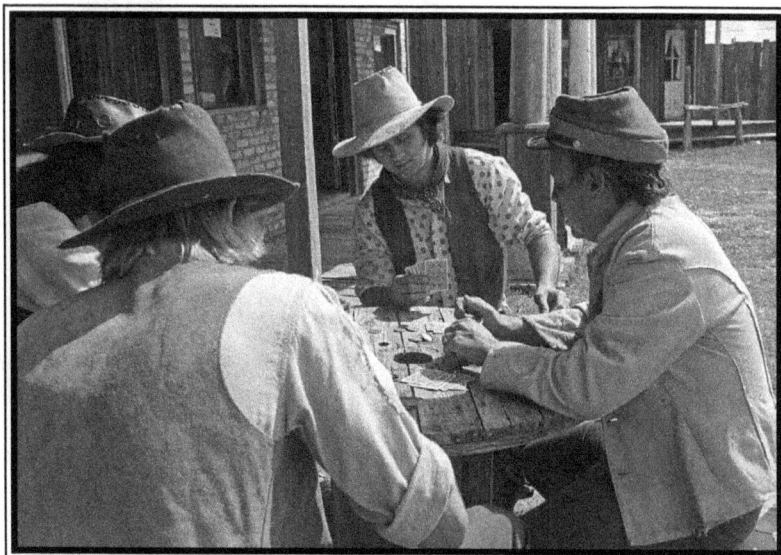

A Couple Hands Of Poker On The Side

A Big Crowd Just Interested In Poker? Or A Good Gunfight?

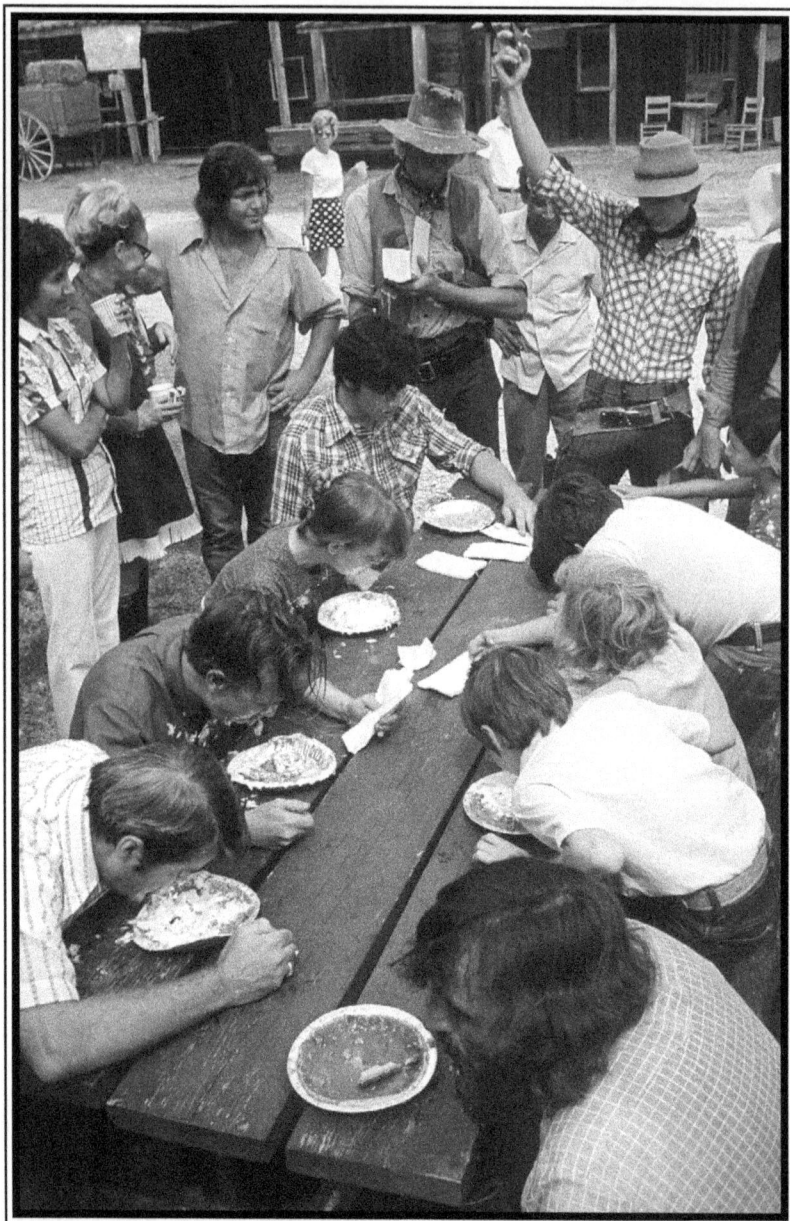

How About A Pie Eating Contest?

Doug, "The Kid" In Charge, Valorie Matthews Joining In

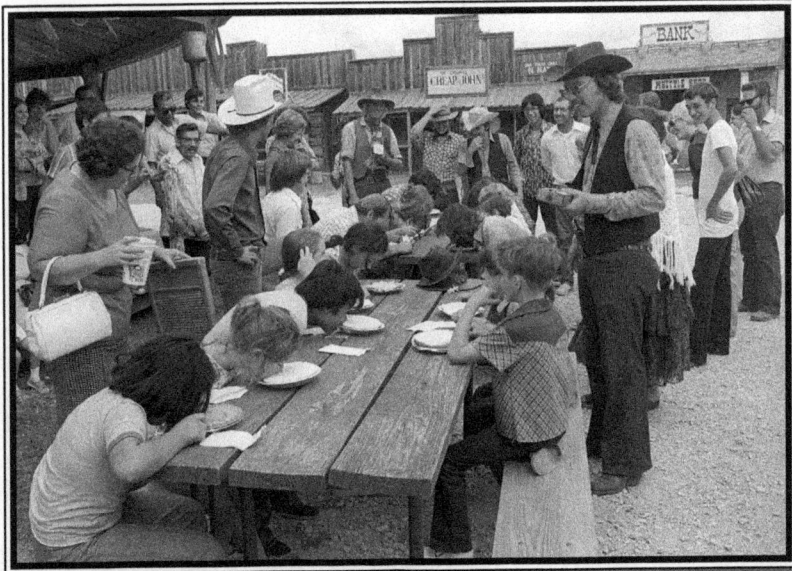

Pie Eating Contest (John Kimbrough Presiding)

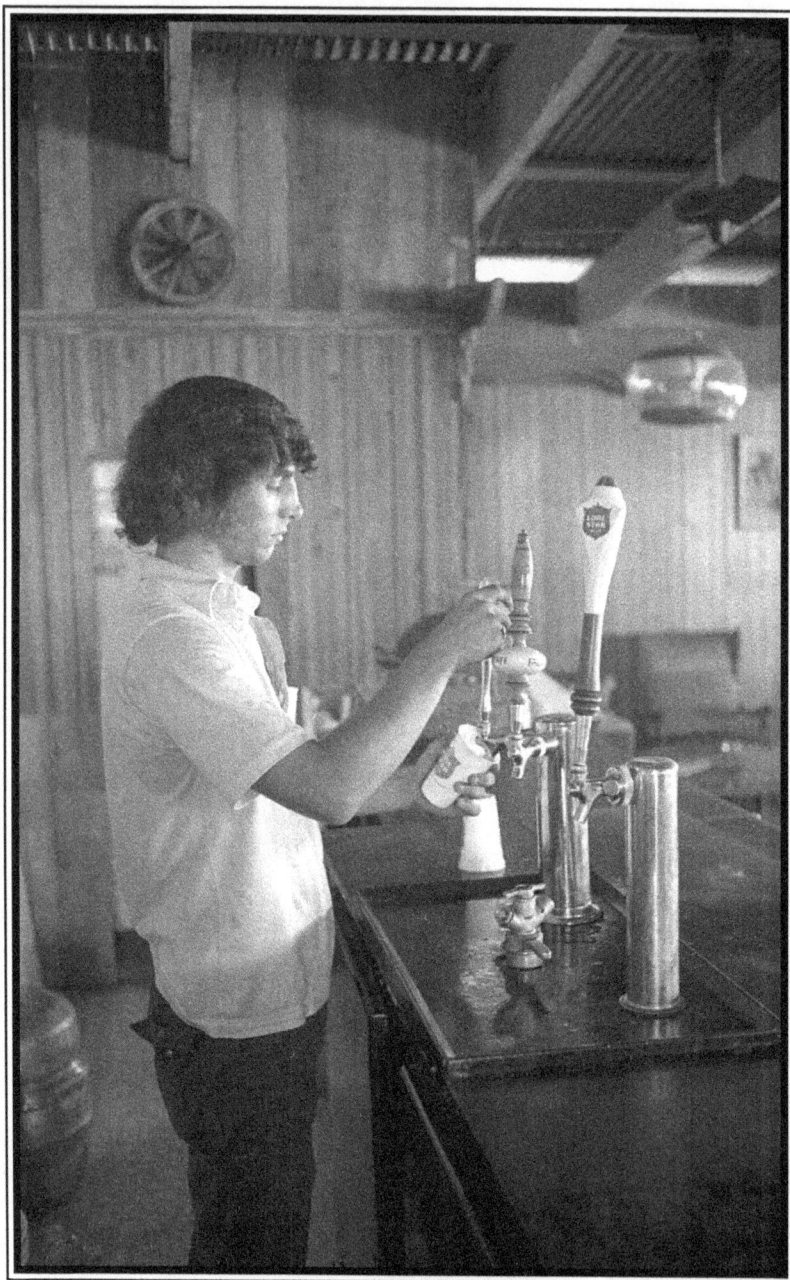

A Bar Serving Real Liquor

A Kitchen Serving Your Choice Of "Period" Foods...

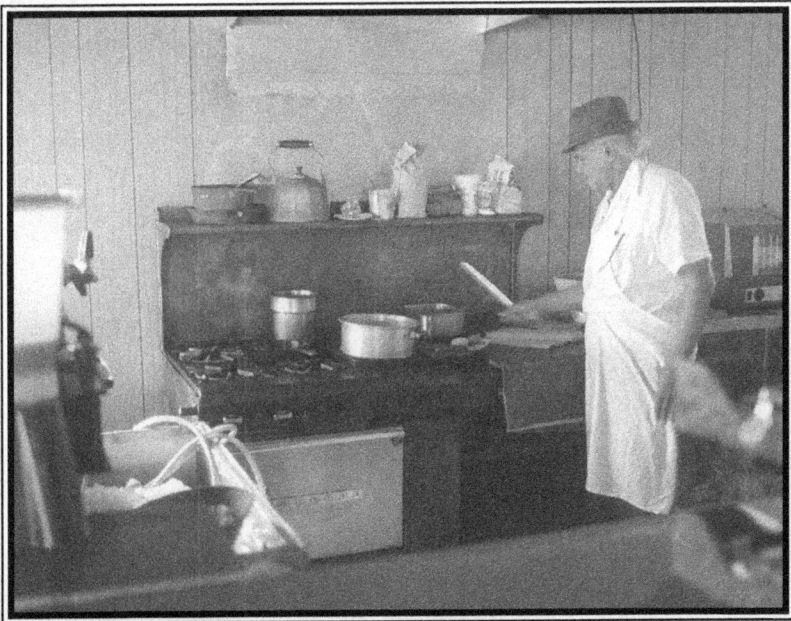

With Wood Stove, Before The Days Of Electric Or Gas

Dusty Ready And Waiting

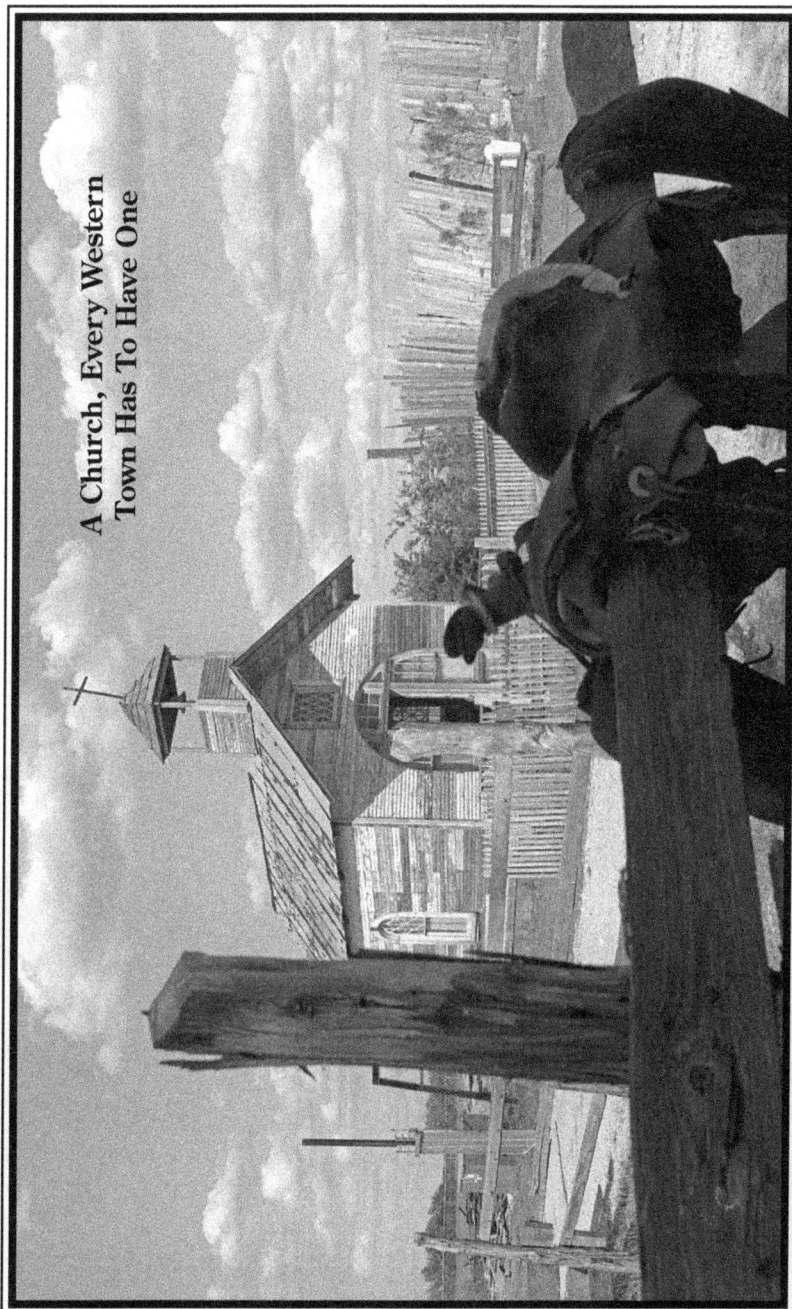

A Church, Every Western Town Has To Have One

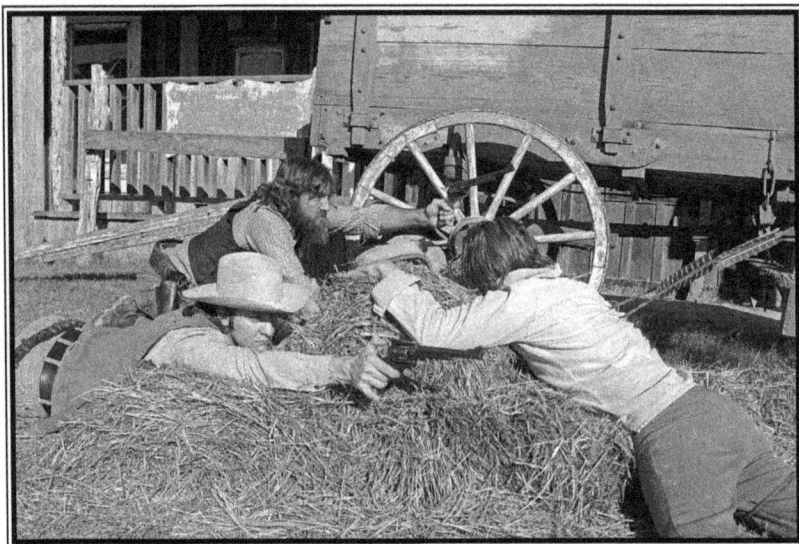

Every Western Town Has To Have Gunfights

Can't Find Your Six-shooter?

A Chicken For Dinner?

Dolly Showing Her Gun Prowess

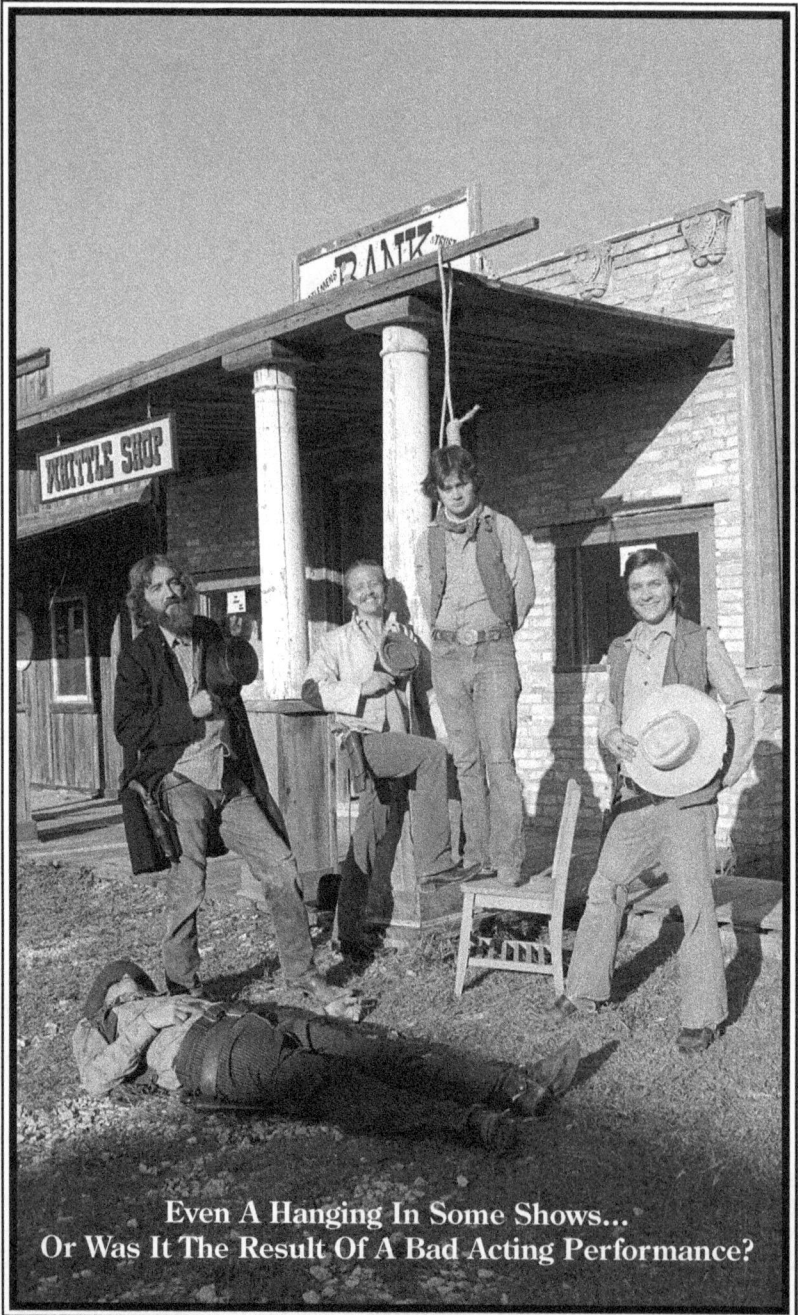

Even A Hanging In Some Shows...
Or Was It The Result Of A Bad Acting Performance?

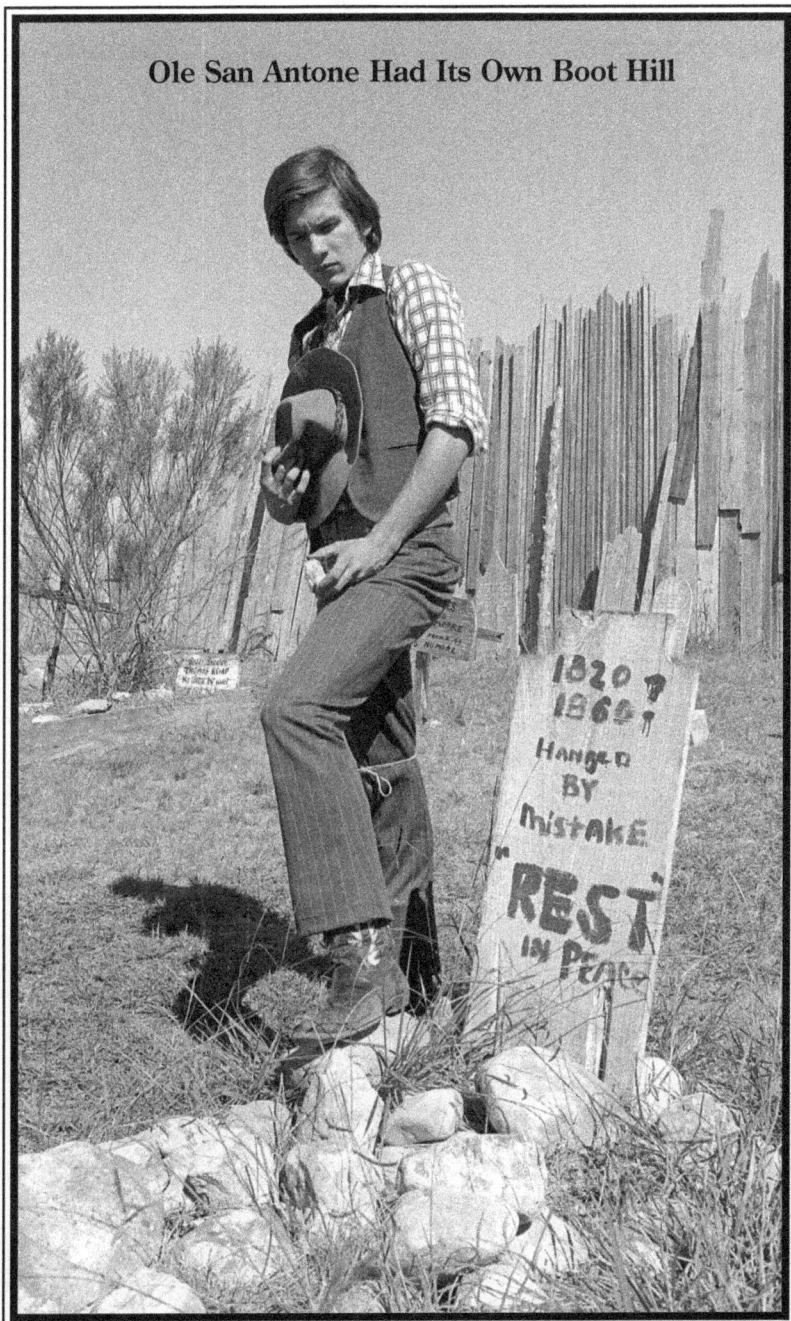

Ole San Antone Had Its Own Boot Hill

1820 ?
1869 ?
HANGED
BY
MISTAKE
"REST"
IN PEACE

CLOSED
On A Rainy Day

www.ingramcontent.com/pod-product-compliance
Lightning Source LLC
Chambersburg PA
CBHW031328040426
42443CB00005B/259